Moses gets a message

DO YOU remember the story of the mother who put her baby boy in a little basket in the river Nile? She wanted to save him from cruel soldiers, so she hid the baby carefully among the reeds.

When the princess of Egypt came to bathe, she heard the baby crying. She soon discovered the boy floating in the basket. She named him Moses and brought him up as a royal prince.

But when he grew up, Moses ran away from Egypt into the desert. There he lived as a shepherd. One day, as he was watching over his sheep, a bush suddenly burst into flames. It burned and burned—but didn't burn away!

Moses was astonished. Then he heard the voice of an angel. "Moses! I want you to go back to Egypt. You must rescue your people, the Hebrews, who are working as slaves for the Egyptians. God says, 'Go to Pharaoh and say, "Let my people go!" Take them out of Egypt.'" Moses was frightened. He didn't like the idea of telling the mighty Pharaoh what to do!

So God promised to help him. "And you can take your brother Aaron too. He can do the talking for both of you!"

So Moses trusted God and set off back to Egypt. He found his brother Aaron and explained what they must do.

Then they set off for Pharaoh's palace. . . .

You can read this story in
Exodus 1:22, 2:2–6

1

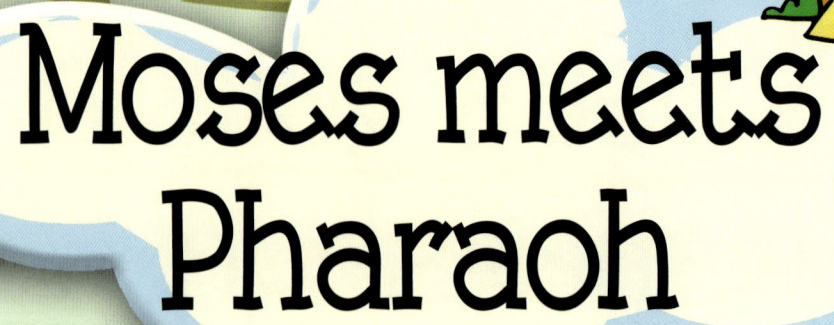

Moses meets Pharaoh

PHARAOH WAS king of Egypt. He was cruel and tough. He didn't like anyone telling *him* what to do.

But Moses and Aaron still went to his palace. They said, "God says, 'Let my people go free!'"

"Oh—does he?" said Pharaoh. And he just ordered his soldiers to make the Hebrews work even *harder*.

The next day Moses and Aaron went back to Pharaoh. This time, Aaron hit the river Nile with his stick. It turned the water red.

"Look how great God is!" said Moses.

But Pharaoh said, "I will never let your people go free!"

So God said to Moses, "Go to Pharaoh *again*. Tell him, if he doesn't let my people go, terrible things will happen."

But still Pharaoh wouldn't let the Hebrews go. So lots of awful things happened in Egypt. All the fish in the rivers died. They made a dreadful smell! Millions of frogs appeared and jumped everywhere. Swarms of flies flew in and bit the Egyptians, all over. Every single cow in Egypt dropped dead. Huge hailstones fell from the sky. Thousands and thousands of greedy locusts jumped across the land and gobbled every last green leaf. The Egyptians were very worried and didn't know what to do.

But then came something even worse. One night, the oldest son in every Egyptian home died.

You can read this story in Exodus 7:8

Moses' people go free

"SOON WE will be able to leave Egypt forever," Moses told the Hebrews. He said "Bake bread quickly to eat on the journey." They ate their supper standing up, so that they were ready to leave as soon as the signal came.

Then Moses and Aaron went to Pharaoh one last time.

"Go now!" said Pharaoh. "You don't know *how* glad I am to see the back of you all!"

It was the middle of the night. The Hebrews picked up their bags, herded together their sheep and goats and cattle, and set off to leave Egypt for ever. They wanted to get away before Pharaoh could change his mind again!

How glad they were to leave behind the long years of being slaves!

Moses explained to the Hebrews that God had a special land for them—the Promised Land. Now they were setting out on a journey to that land.

At first the Hebrews were happy to be going. They sang as they marched. They no longer had to work as slaves.

But the Egyptians were angry, because now they had nobody to work for them.

You can read this story in Exodus 12:1–39

3

At the Red Sea

THEN THE *worst* thing happened—Pharaoh changed his mind.

"Why ever did I let all those Hebrew slaves go?" he said.

Pharaoh called for his generals. "Follow those miserable Hebrews," he roared. "I want every single one dragged back to Egypt."

The Hebrews had marched a long way. In front of them lay the gleaming waters of the Red Sea. Then they saw Pharaoh's army racing after them.

Their hearts stopped. How would they possibly get across the Red Sea? They were trapped! Sure as anything, Pharaoh would catch them all and take them back to Egypt to become slaves again.

Then God said to Moses, "Stretch out your arm."

Moses did so. That very moment, the waters pushed back, and a dry path appeared across the sea. The water made two walls.

Without another word, the Hebrews marched across—between the waters of the Red Sea—until they were all safely across, every one of them.

But even as they reached safety, the Egyptians were following them along the dry path between the waters. Then, suddenly the sea crashed down on the Egyptians. But all the Hebrews were safe!

You can read this story in Exodus 14:5–31

4

MIDIAN

EGYPT

GOSHEN

RED SEA

Using the stickers, can you complete the map? Use the place names as a guide.

SINAI PENINSULA

KADESH BARNEA

MOUNT SINAI

MOUNT NEBO

Using the stickers, can you complete the map? Use the place names as a guide.

Special food to eat

THE HEBREWS marched on and on. At night, God gave them a special pillar of fire to lead the way. By day, they had a pillar of cloud to show them where to go.

On and on they marched. But it was terribly hot under the burning sun. And the Hebrews weren't used to marching. Soon the grumbling started.

"Do you remember the luscious fruit we used to have in Egypt?" people asked.

" . . . and the wonderful cakes and bread!"

"Do you remember the pomegranates and melons, the onions and cucumbers?"
On and on they grumbled.

Moses told God about the moaning. So every morning, God sent a special food called manna. It lay thick on the ground when the people woke up. They went out and gathered it—there was always enough for that day.

And in the evening, God sent little birds called quails. The Hebrews caught the quails and cooked and ate them. And, at least for a time, the grumbling stopped, because God had given his people special food—manna and quails.

But because of the moaning and grumbling, it was many, many years before the Hebrews even *saw* the Promised Land.

You can read this story in Exodus 16:4, 13–18

5

Moses climbs a mountain

AND SO the Hebrews trudged on through the desert, until at long last they reached a high mountain called Mount Sinai. Moses climbed to the very top of Mount Sinai.

On Mount Sinai Moses met God. When he climbed down again, he carried two great, flat stones. On the stones were carved ten very special rules, rules that God had given the Hebrews.

The rules are often called the "Ten Commandments." God wrote things like, "I am the One God" and "Be good to your mother and father" and "Don't steal someone else's things."

But Moses was away so long on Mount Sinai that the Hebrews thought he was lost and wasn't coming back. So Aaron made a calf out of gold.

"Let's worship the golden calf," he said. "Moses is lost—and we don't know how to speak to God!"

Then at last Moses came down the mountain. When he saw the golden calf, he was so angry that he smashed the stones to pieces. He had to go right back up Mount Sinai to ask God for two brand new stones with the Rules.

The Hebrews told God they were sorry for making the calf. They made a special golden box to keep the Ten Commandments in. It had handles, so when they marched on, they could take the box with them.

You can read this story in Exodus 20:1–17, 32:1–6, 15–19

Moses sees the Promised Land

AFTER MANY, many years wandering in the desert, and lots more adventures, the Hebrews came to another mountain. It was called Mount Nebo.

They stood with Moses on the top of the mountain, and way, way in the distance at last they could see the land that God had promised them.

Moses was very old now. He had been a prince of Egypt. Then a shepherd in the desert. And now he had led his people, the Hebrews, through the desert for many years.

But Moses had done some wrong things. So he himself could not go to the Promised Land.

After Moses died, a new leader—Joshua—led the Hebrews into the Promised Land.

They carried the golden box with the Ten Commandments across the river Jordan. At last they arrived in the Promised Land!

And in the Promised Land they had many more adventures. They captured Jericho. They had to fight many enemies.

But now God's people had a land of their own—as God had promised.

You can read this story in Numbers 27:18–23; Deuteronomy 34:1–12

The spies' report

AS THEY got nearer to the Promised Land, Moses picked twelve men to go and explore. He sent them to the Promised Land to find out more about it. They were spies. Their job was to discover if it was a good place to live.

Ten of the spies came back shivering with fear. "The land is full of fierce giants!" they said. "We felt like grasshoppers when we saw them. We can never beat these people! We can't have this land."

But two of the spies came back carrying an enormous bunch of grapes. The bunch was so big, they had to hang it from a carrying-pole and put it on their shoulders.

These two spies were called Caleb and Joshua.

"The Promised Land is full of fruit and other good food," they said. "It is green and has flowing rivers. It will be a wonderful place to live."

But lots of the Hebrews were too scared to go to the Promised Land because they had heard the people there were giants!

It was still many years before the Hebrews reached the land that God had promised them.

You can read this story in Numbers 13:2, 23, 27